MANDALAS
Mini Adult Coloring Book

http://www.KipADoodles.com

ISBN: 1-886522-07-3
ISBN-13: 978-1-886522-07-7

Your Free Gift...

Want some free adult coloring pages? Want access to more freebies and special offers from Kip aDoodles?

As a way of saying thanks for your purchase of this coloring book, I'm offering **THREE FREE** adult coloring Mandala designs which are available only to my fellow color-ers! These pages are not sold anywhere else and can only be found via subscription.

Plus you will receive THREE NEW FREE adult coloring pages every month. And you will receive instant notification whenever I release a new coloring book, along with the chance to receive designs available *only* through my website. Finally, you will receive special discounts on all of my books!

Subscribe to my Email Newsletter and Download Your First FREE Pages Now!

Get the details here:

http://www.kipadoodles.com/subscribe

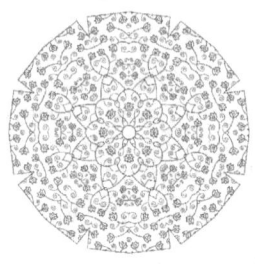 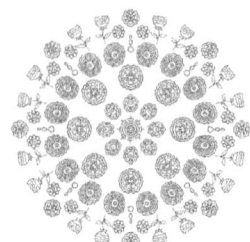 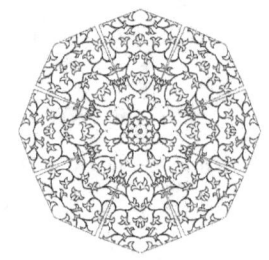

How To Enjoy This Book

Welcome to this Kip aDoodles coloring book!

START ANYWHERE! Begin coloring on the page that captures your attention. If it's the first design, last design, or somewhere else in the book – that's the perfect place to begin your journey!

TAKE YOUR TIME! There is no race, no competition, no schedule. There are no "right" or "wrong" ways to color these designs. You don't even have to stay within in the lines! The only rule is that you have fun!

Coloring is a chance to release your inner child, to go back to those innocent days of youth. Coloring is also a great stress reliever! It is relaxing, meditative, and best of all, actual restful for your brain. In fact, by engaging the right side of your brain (the creative side), it can help your cognitive health!

You'll have hours of fun, mindful calm and relaxation while you color the 25 original mandala designs in this coloring book. Each design is just waiting for you to bring it to life with color! Escape for a few minutes or hours at a time.

The designs in this book range in complexity, but there is nothing too intricate for even a beginning colorist to enjoy. Printed on individual pages for easy coloring offers you two benefits: The coloring will not bleed through and ruin another picture. And your finished work of art can be removed and framed, if you want to.

Easily color these designs with any dry media, like colored pencils or crayons. You can also color with gel pens or markers. If you decide to use gel pens, markers or another form of wet media, I recommend that you put an extra piece of paper or even poster board behind the design you're working on. This will ensure the wet media will not bleed through to other designs. With the more intricate designs, you might consider using ultra-fine pens or markers to easily color the smaller design areas.

Share the experience! Have you ever colored with your family or a friend? Or with a group? Discover the joy of sharing the phenomenon of coloring! Some communities even have coloring groups who regularly meet. What fun is that!

Please "Like" my Facebook page https://www.facebook.com/kipadoodles and share your completed artwork. Seeing how the designs come to life in your hands will be great fun!

IMPORTANT: **Please do not re-sell these images.** If you are interested in licensing my art or any type of commercial, educational or non-profit use, please email me at Kip@KipADoodles.com. I would love to hear from you!

Any questions or suggestions? Don't hesitate to email me Kip@KipADoodles.com.

Happy coloring!

Kip@KipADoodles.com

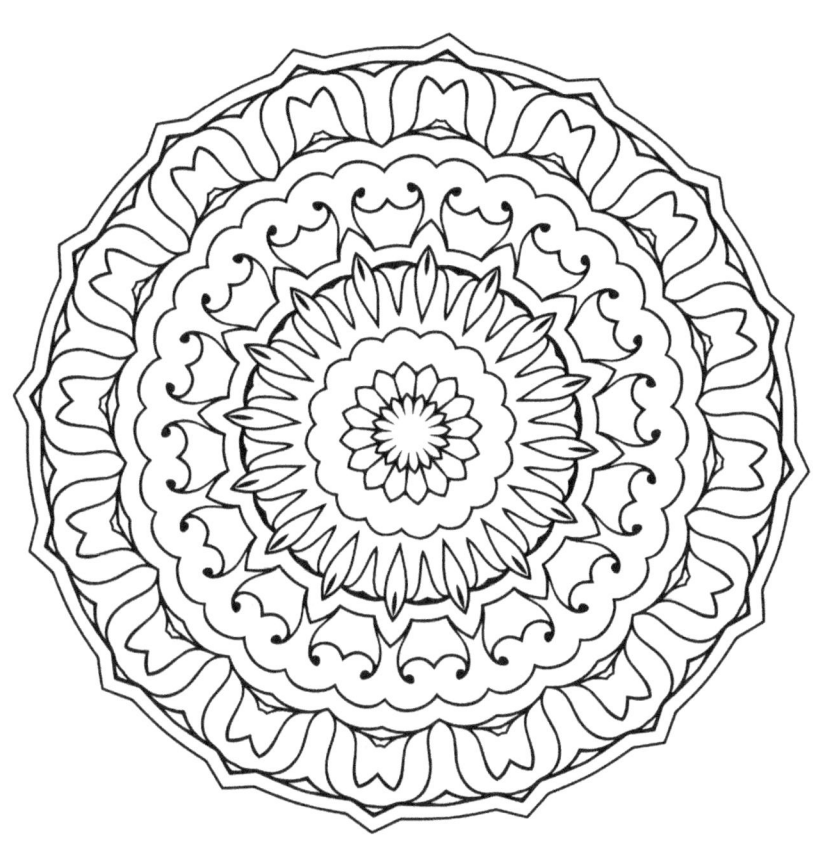

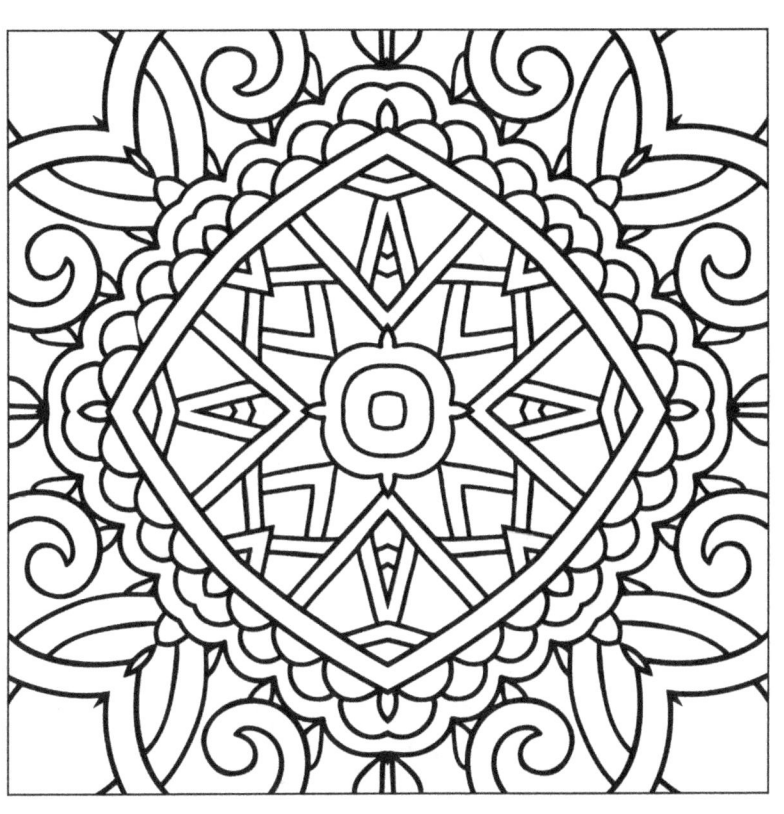

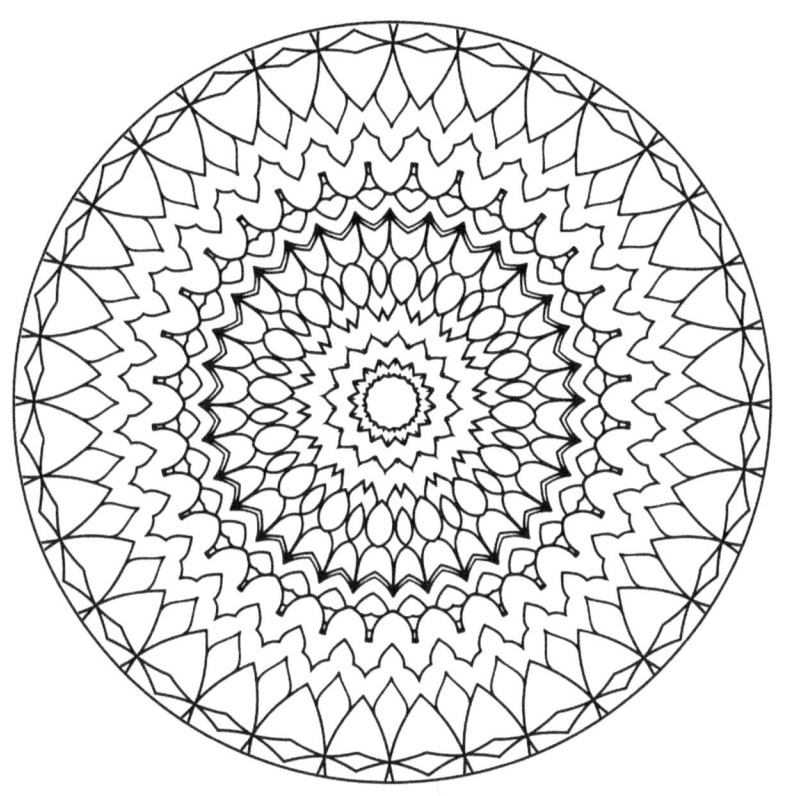

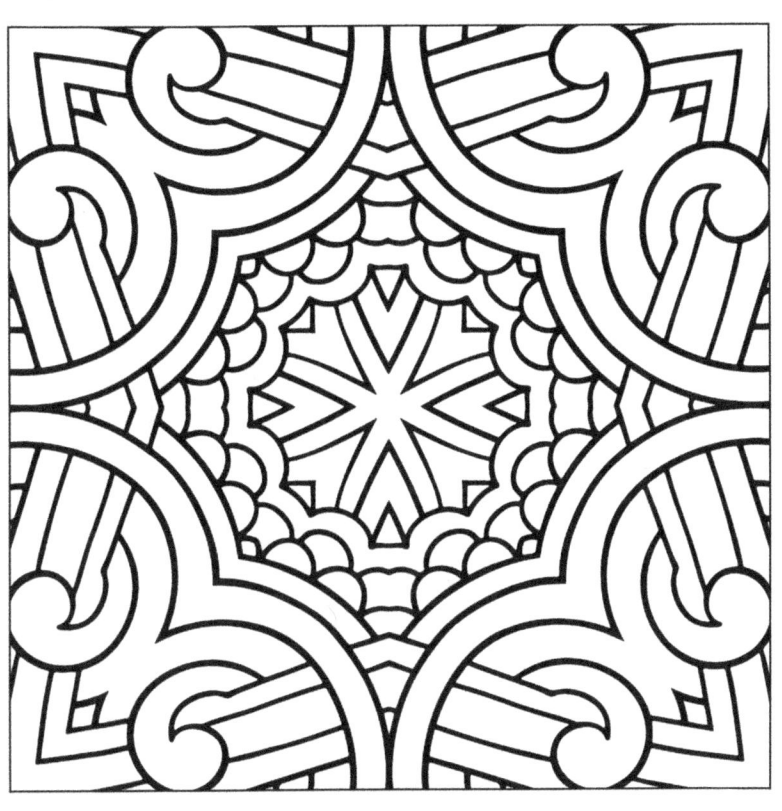

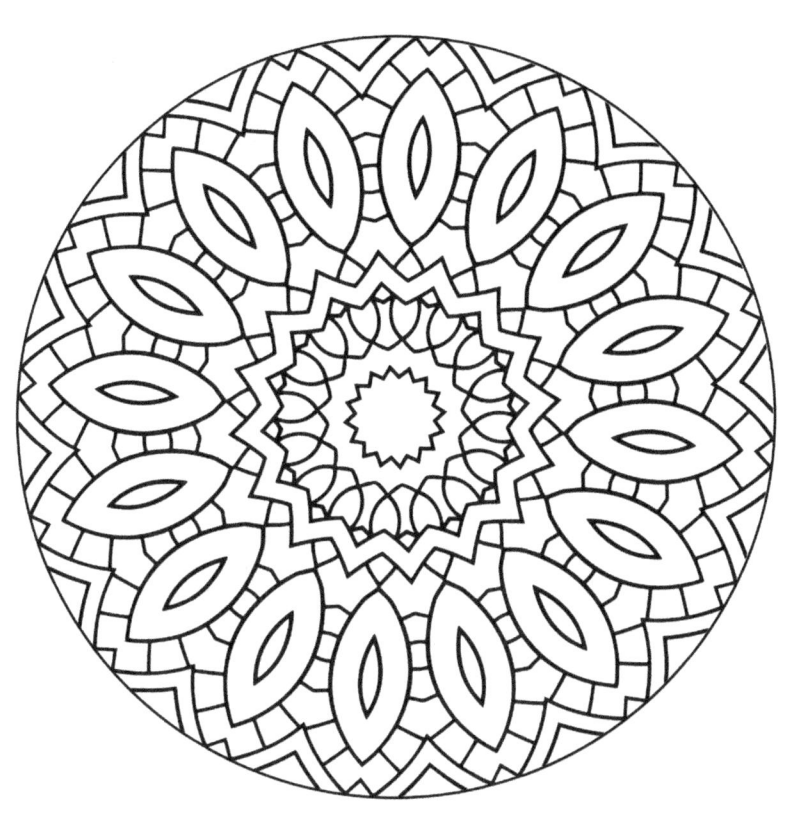

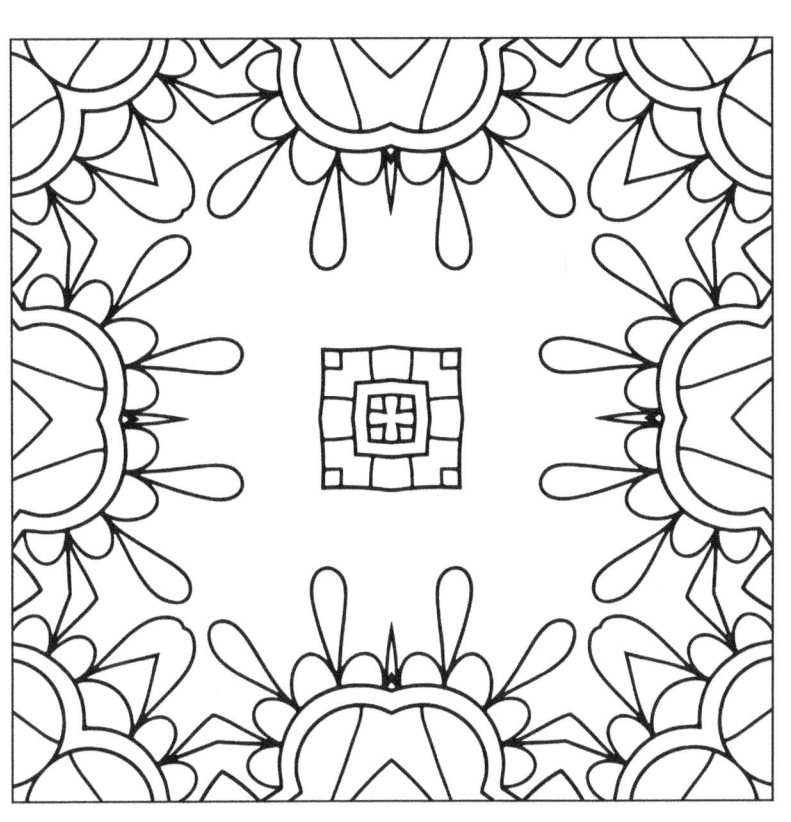

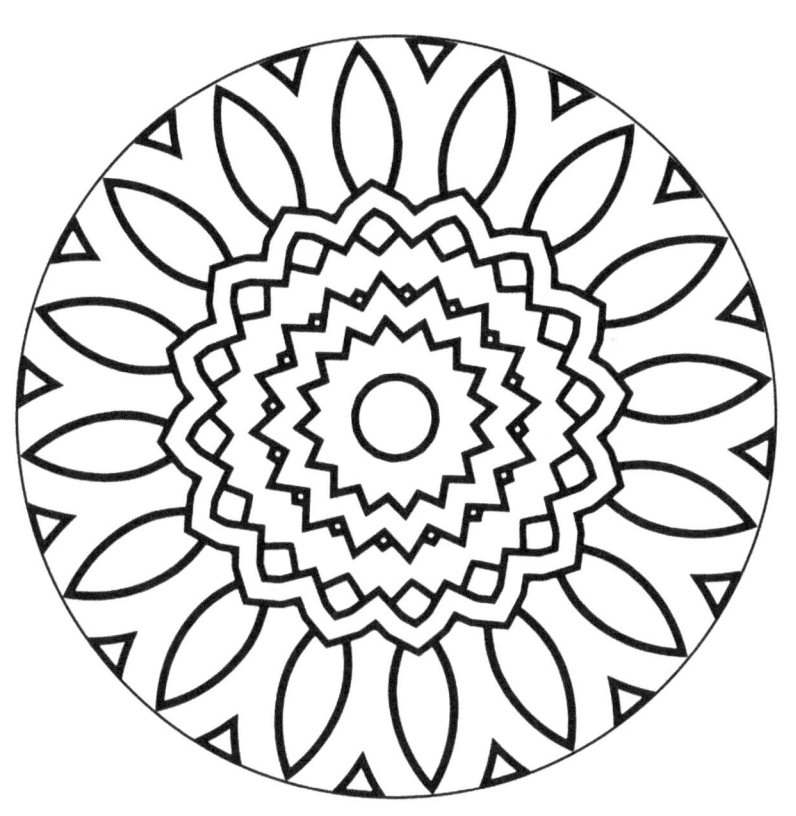

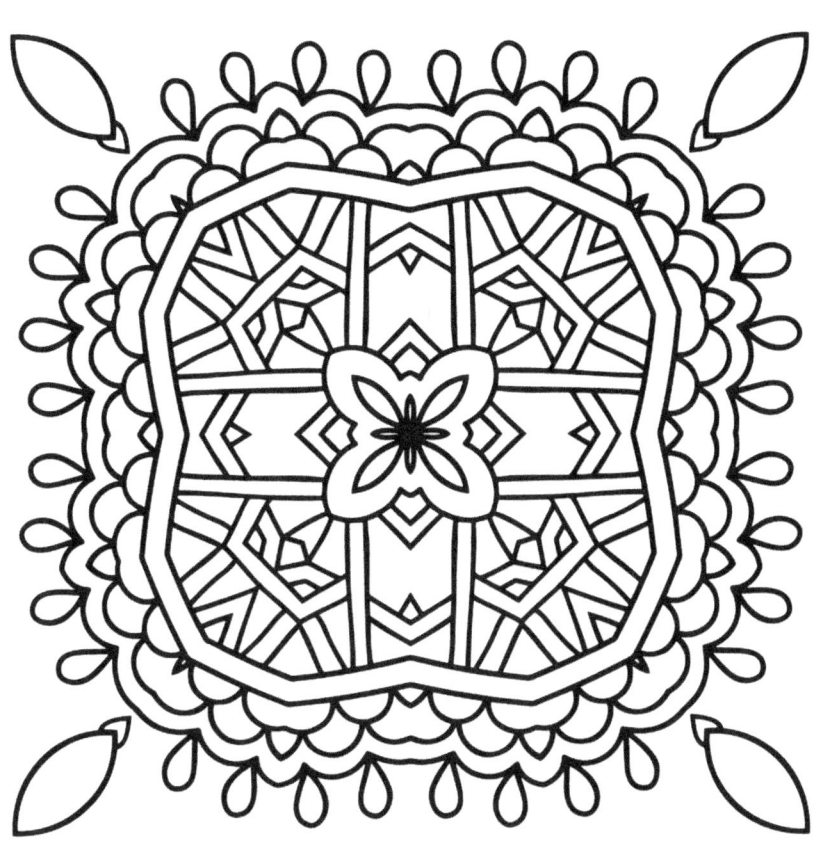

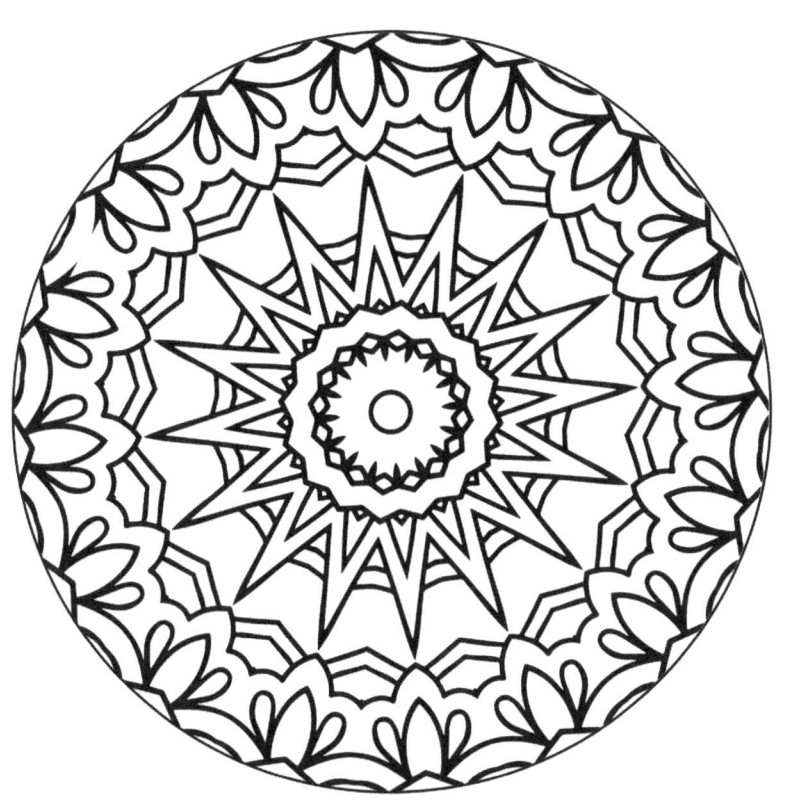

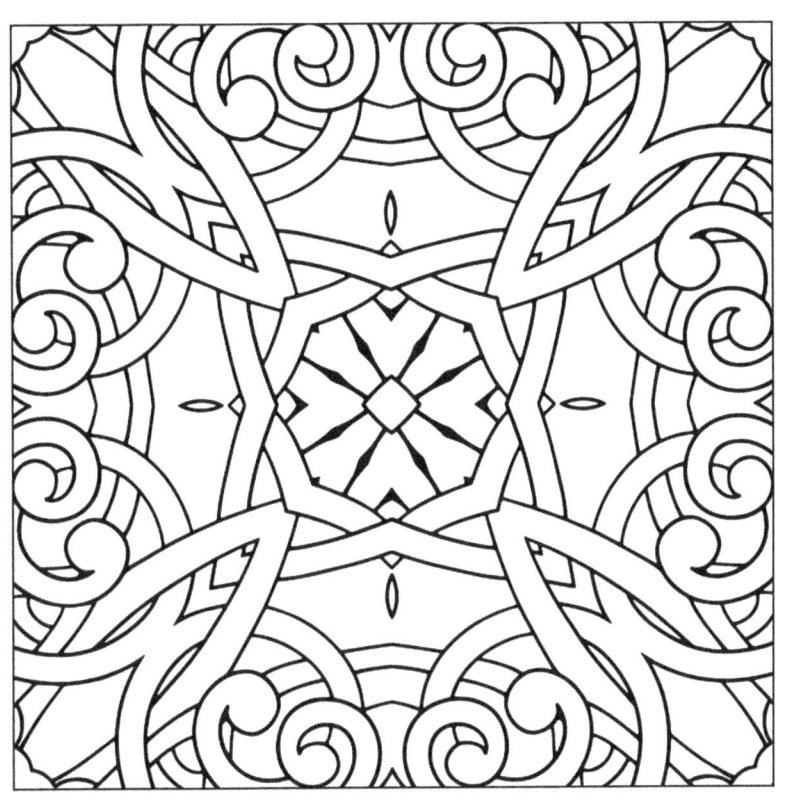

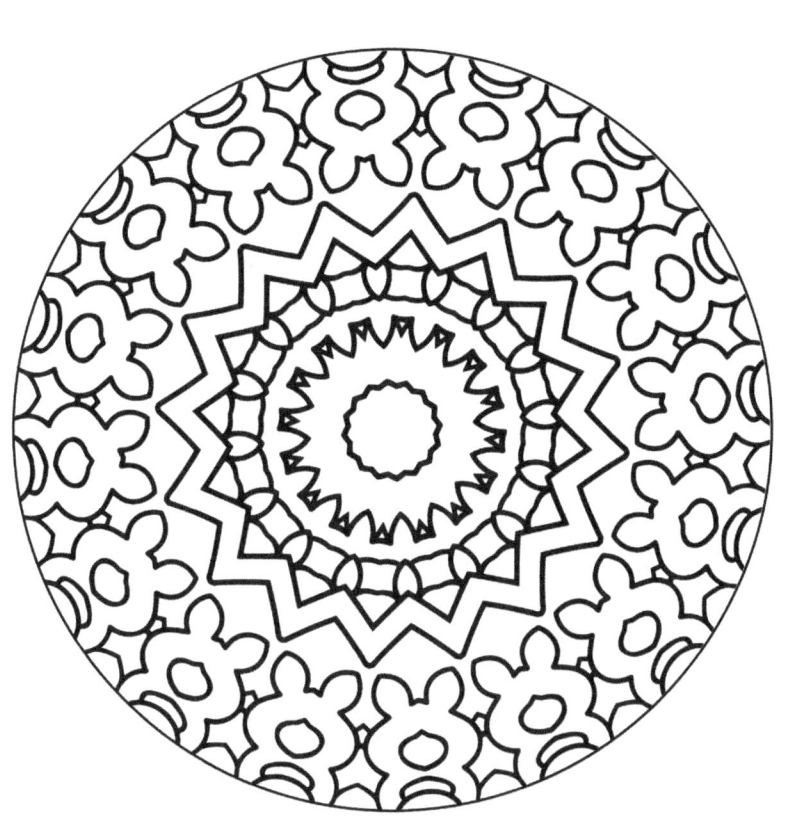

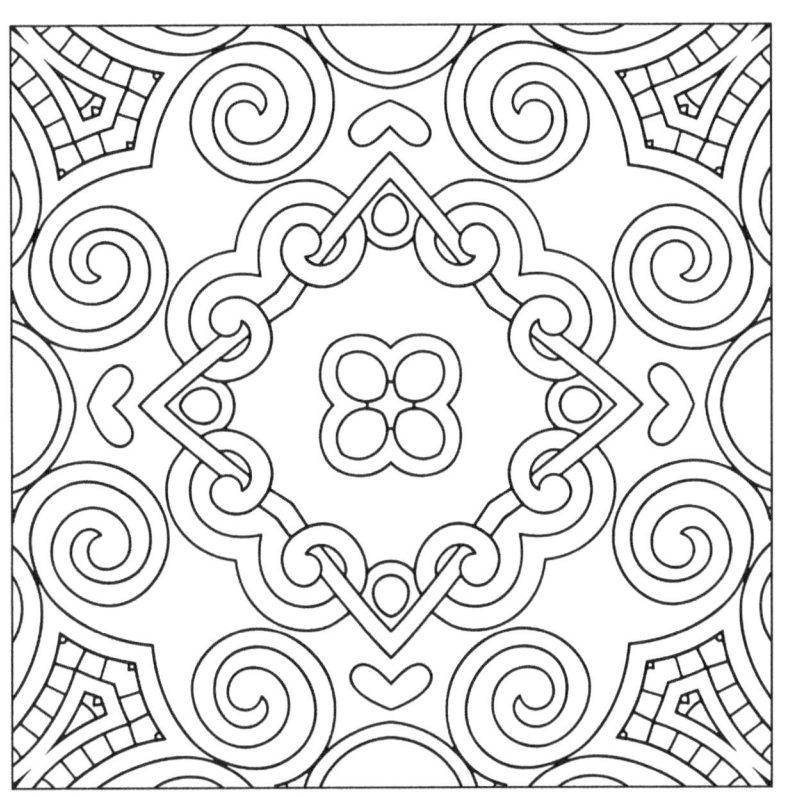

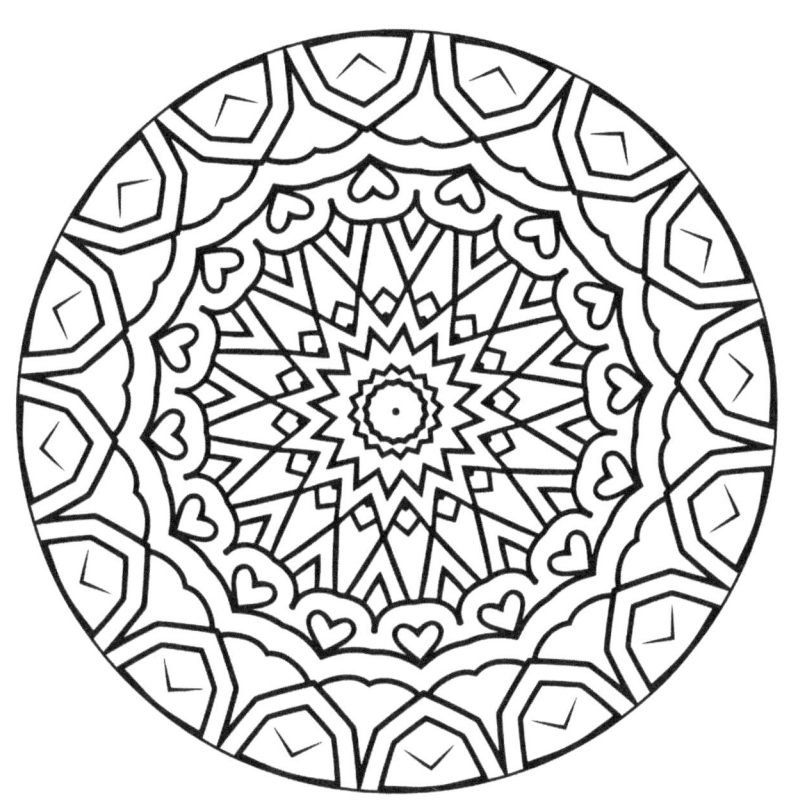